IMAGES
of America

FARGO
NORTH DAKOTA

1870–1940

IMAGES
of America

FARGO
NORTH DAKOTA
1870–1940

David B. Danbom & Claire Strom

with help from Jennifer Grosz & John R. Hallberg

ARCADIA
PUBLISHING

Published by Arcadia Publishing
Charleston, South Carolina

Library of Congress Catalog Card Number: 2002108559

For all general information contact Arcadia Publishing at:
Telephone 843-853-2070
Fax 843-853-0044
E-mail sales@arcadiapublishing.com
For customer service and orders:
Toll-Free 1-888-313-2665

Visit us on the Internet at www.arcadiapublishing.com

CONTENTS

ACKNOWLEDGMENTS

We wish to thank John Hallberg and Jen Grosz for helping us find and identify the images in this book. Erin Strehlo, Jessica Holkup, and Erik Lorntson provided useful research information. The book was facilitated by a grant from the Office of Sponsored Programs Administration at North Dakota State University, which we appreciate. Finally, we thank Jim Norris for suggesting the project, and Arcadia Publishing for their help and encouragement, especially our editor, Samantha Gleisten.

PHOTO CREDITS
John R. Hallberg, Fargo, ND
David Smith, Fargo, ND
North Dakota Institute for Regional Studies
State Historical Society of North Dakota

INTRODUCTION

Fargo, North Dakota, is one of America's many success stories. It is a place that, during the period portrayed in these pages, went from virtually open prairie to a city of 35,000; from a spot along the Red River of the North to the central town in a large and prosperous agricultural region.

Fargo's success was due partly to luck. The city grew at the place where the Northern Pacific decided to bridge the Red, a reality reflected in one of the city's nicknames—the "Gateway to the Northwest." The railroad assured the town's existence, but not its prominence.

But Fargo's success was also the product of design. In the early years it benefited from the attention of a number of entrepreneurial boosters who linked their fortunes to its star. These men, mostly Yankees and Canadians, grew wealthy by building a city, selling real estate, and lending money. They multiplied Fargo's advantages by attracting other railroads, extending the city's reach in new directions, and winning cheaper shipping rates than its regional competitors enjoyed. The city's transportation advantages made it the retail, wholesale, and service center for a vast region.

Fargo's success drew people. Immigrants poured into the city. Many were from Norway—so many, in fact, that Fargo was a bi-lingual city until World War I—but others came from Sweden, Germany, Ireland, Poland, Lithuania, Russia, and a number of other places. These immigrants brought numerous cultural traditions, languages, and religions—particularly Lutheranism, but also Catholicism and Judaism.

Other migrants came from surrounding areas. Young men and women moved into Fargo from the farms and villages of North Dakota and Western Minnesota, drawn by the bright lights of what seemed like an exciting place, by the educational opportunities available there, and by the numerous jobs in retail, wholesale, manufacturing, construction, and personal service that the city offered.

People came to Fargo to enjoy the good life, but they did not define that solely in material terms. They were determined to build a city in which people wanted to live, and not just one that benefited them economically. Fargoans constructed impressive churches and a school system few cities could equal; they built hospitals and demonstrated a strong commitment to public health; they created a park system and recreational facilities; and they developed an intricate infrastructure of clubs, service organizations, and lodges. Fargo was a city of organizations, as well as of individuals.

Despite Fargo's success, it still faced challenges. It was devastated by a fire in 1893 that destroyed over half the structures in the city, and by a record-setting flood in 1897. The city coped with the vagaries of the weather and the river. And it faced resentment from people in the surrounding areas, who envied its success and considered it smug and arrogant. Some of these challenges the city learned to live with; others—like the Great Fire—it overcame. Challenges overcome were a source of pride for the place that proudly styled itself the "Queen City" of the Northern Plains.

So the pages that follow are mainly a chronicle of success. They illustrate the story of the creation of Fargo, its growth, and its rise to significance in a sparsely populated region. Some of the buildings and artifacts of those early days are with us still. We hope that the images and text of this book will help bring them to life in the minds and memories of our readers.

One

FOUNDATIONS

The human history of Fargo, North Dakota, extends back many hundreds of years. Native Americans used the Red River and its banks as a source of food and the river itself as a means of travel. When Euro-American fur traders first arrived in the mid-nineteenth century, the area around Fargo had no permanent occupants. Instead, it was contested ground between the Ojibwe or Chippewa from further east and the Dakota or Sioux to the west.

Like the American Indians, Euro-Americans were first attracted to the area by its wildlife and transportation potential. The Red River became a major artery in the fur trade. French-Canadian and Métis fur traders walked Red River ox carts, laden with furs, down the river and then to St. Paul, making that city, by the 1830s, one of the largest fur markets in the country. Most of these people lived in the northern end of the Valley, between Pembina and Winnipeg. As traders in St. Paul sought better access to the rich furs, they explored new transportation options, including river traffic and railroads. The Northern Pacific railroad that led to the founding of Fargo, however, was not built to ship furs out of the Valley, but rather was always intended as a transcontinental line.

In 1871, the Northern Pacific Railroad chose Moorhead, Minnesota, as the place to bridge the Red River. This attracted large numbers of construction workers and other squatters to both banks. These men, like these in front of the office of bridge builders, lived in rough conditions, sleeping in shacks and tents. (NDIRS, Mss 1970.134)

Through much of the 1870s, St. Paul entrepreneurs such as Norman Kittson and James J. Hill brought furs down the Red River on steamboats. These were cheaper but less efficient than trains, but were limited by the course of the river and the season of the year. (NDIRS, 51.51.17)

On June 6, 1872, Charles Cotter drove the first train across the Red River and into Dakota Territory. The arrival of the railroad guaranteed the development of settlements on both sides of the river. (NDIRS, 51.62.1)

The early construction and surveying crews lived in a tent city on the prairie. Banned from "Fargo on the Prairie" by Northern Pacific supervisors, liquor dealers, prostitutes, and other rowdy elements, they settled along the river in "Fargo in the Timber." (NDIRS, Mss 1970.13.12)

The Hector House was the first permanent house in Fargo and was originally constructed in present-day Island Park. The house has since been moved to the Cass County Historical Society museum at Bonanzaville. (NDIRS, Mss 1970.23.7)

In 1873, Jay Cooke's banking house collapsed as a result of overselling Northern Pacific bonds. The collapse brought down the railroad, too, and plunged the entire country into a financial depression. Although the Northern Pacific did continue to run, its bankruptcy significantly affected its operations. New construction was decidedly limited, and it was unclear if the railroad was ever going to reach its goal of the West Coast. (NDIRS, 328.1.10)

The railroad did survive and did reach the Pacific. Meanwhile, Fargo slowly attracted more settlers who worked for the railway and in the nascent agricultural business. (NDIRS, 2029.8.19)

When the railroad rebounded and started to prosper, the Headquarters Hotel was built in Fargo. This hotel served as the main hostelry in the town and center for civic life until 1897, when it burned down. The impressive building was intended to signify permanence and success to potential settlers. (NDIRS, 51.38.12)

13

In the 1870s and 1880s, many Fargoans still lived in shacks, like these on Front Street, now Main Avenue, in 1879, giving the city a contingent and transient appearance. (NDIRS, 2042.29.6)

The center of town was platted in anticipation of considerable growth. Buildings in this 1880 photograph, including one made of brick, are widely spaced, demonstrating the inhabitants' optimism that the Fargo boom would continue. (NDIRS, 2029.8.25)

James Holes, who crossed the river by ferry in July 1871, was one of the city's earliest settlers. Coming upon a tent, he found a man sitting in the shade playing a waltz on a violin while a woman danced. They were Captain and Mrs. George Egbert. The Captain later became Fargo's first mayor, while Holes made a considerable fortune in farming and real estate. (NDIRS, 2068.1.1)

In April 1875, with Fargo recently incorporated by the Dakota Territorial Legislature, the first City Government Council meeting convened in this office. Present were the newly elected aldermen of the city: W.D. Maddocks, A.C. Kvello, P.H. McCarthy, E.A. Grant, George A. Strout, and the owner of the office, attorney Samuel G. Roberts. Fargo retained the council form of government until 1913, when it adopted a city commission. (NDIRS, 2041.21.12)

While the Fargo post office looked urban enough in 1876, getting the mail was still a challenge. In the 1870s, Matt Hammes of Lisbon, North Dakota, had the contract to transport mail to and from Grand Forks. He made the trip three times a week, using stage coaches or ponies in the summer, but often resorting to a dog sled during winter storms. (NDIRS, 2029.8.40)

One of the first brick structures in the city was the Stephens and Sears Livery Barn, seen here in 1880. Note the Fargo Omnibus Line coach in the foreground—public transportation, 1880-style. (NDIRS, 2029.8.22)

The building at the far right is the studio of photographer F. Jay Haynes that opened in 1879. Haynes, who came to the area in 1876, traveled throughout Dakota Territory and the West, photographing places and people for the Northern Pacific. He was one of the first photographers to visit Yellowstone. (NDIRS, 2042.4.9)

In 1879, James Holes built this beautiful Italianate house, which is still standing. The house demonstrated both the permanence and prosperity of the young town. (NDIRS, 2068.2.4)

As the city grew, so did its infrastructure of public services. The first public school in Fargo was housed in "a rickety wooden shack" on a lot donated by the Northern Pacific. One of the first teachers, Miss Elvina Pinkham, taught from 1874 to 1878. She was paid $50 a month. At the end of her time, she had 60 pupils, and a new building had to be found. Therefore, the school board rented the Methodist church for $5 a month. (NDIRS, 2029.8.31)

Two

TRANSPORTATION

Transportation was vital to Fargo, as to all cities. Although the area was initially connected to the wider world by the Red River, it was the arrival of the railroad that really established the community on the river's western bank. Inhabitants of Fargo were well-aware of the city's railroad origins and their continued economic dependence on the Northern Pacific. Thus, although the town was originally called Centralia, in 1872 the name was changed in honor of William G. Fargo, the founder of Wells Fargo Express and, more importantly, a member of the Northern Pacific Board of Directors.

As the bonanza farm boom took hold in the 1870s and 1880s throughout the Red River Valley, the Great Northern and later the Milwaukee Road established connections to Fargo. These lines took the agricultural bounty of the Valley to market, usually in the Twin Cities, and brought back goods for the frontier citizens of Fargo and the surrounding region.

As the town increased in size, internal transportation became an issue. With livery stables offering rental horses and carriages in the early years, the city tried to install a horse-drawn streetcar in the late 1870s and early 1880s. This failed, but in 1904, Fargo followed many other cities by constructing an electric streetcar system. Private transportation in the city also followed national trends, with a brief interest in bicycling at the turn of the century, giving way to the American love affair with the automobile.

In 1882, the St. Paul, Minneapolis, & Manitoba Railroad ran through Fargo. The line was renamed the Great Northern Railway in 1889. (NDIRS, 2065.27.2)

The railroads opened up the Red River Valley and the Great Plains for commercial agriculture. Without the trains, farmers would have been unable to get their produce to market. However, this dependence bred resentment, as farmers opposed railroad monopolies and price gouging. Towns such as Fargo, located as rural hubs, often found themselves caught in the battle between their two major economic resources: railroads and farmers. (NDIRS, 2029.8.30)

In 1880, the F. Jay Haynes studio took this photograph of the Northern Pacific's freight house with delivery wagons parked outside it on Front Street, now Main Avenue. (NDIRS, 2029.8.26)

The Northern Pacific passenger depot was completed in 1900. The depot was designed by Cass Gilbert, who was also the architect for the Minnesota State Capitol and the Woolworth building in New York. Originally housing two fireplaces and a restaurant, the depot's use diminished with the decline of passenger travel on railways after World War II. The depot is now home to a Senior Citizens' Center and Park Board offices. (John R. Hallberg)

Trying to reduce railroad rates, some Fargo businessmen decided to build their own line to link up with the Chicago, Milwaukee, and St. Paul Railroad (later the Milwaukee Road). They completed the Fargo and Southern in 1884. The line was bought out by the Milwaukee, which ran passenger service through Fargo from this depot until 1956. (NDIRS, 2070.262.1)

Samuel Bartlett, a friend of railroad president James J. Hill, designed the Great Northern depot. The 1906 building was constructed in the popular Richardsonian Romanesque style that Hill had commissioned for his own house on St. Paul's Summit Avenue. (NDIRS, 2023.86.1)

In the early years of the city, both public and private transportation was by horse or on foot. Thus carriage makers often achieved both economic and political importance. William Mills, pictured far right, painted and trimmed carriages for a living and also served as Fargo's Police Department Commissioner in the 1890s. (NDIRS, 2029.8.32)

The first automobile in Fargo made its appearance in 1897. Initially, people were dubious about the safety and efficiency of autos. One of the big concerns in Fargo was whether the machines would run in the snow. (NDIRS, 51.3.1)

Cities throughout the United States started adopting electric streetcars in the late 1880s as a way to deal with urban growth. Streetcar service began in Fargo in 1904 and continued until 1937 (this picture of track repair was taken in 1922). The initial fare was 5¢ per ride, and the cars ran from 6 a.m. to midnight. (NDIRS, 2063.29.28)

The streetcars of Fargo, equipped with electric light and water heat, were mainly used by the middle classes. The poor walked, while wealthier citizens had their own carriages and autos. (NDIRS, 51.193.2)

By the 1920s, Fargoans used a wide variety of transportation methods, including trucks, tractors, cars, streetcars, trains, and perambulators. (NDIRS, 2023.3.18)

In 1908, Henry Ford introduced the Model T, the car for the masses. The immense demand for this car led him to develop assembly line production which further reduced costs. Consequently, by the 1920s, cars had been adopted en masse by middle-class Americans who valued the freedom they offered. (NDIRS, 51.183.3)

Like the rest of the country, Fargo took to automobiles, and parking quickly became a problem in downtown, as this view of Front Street demonstrates. (NDIRS, 51.142.1)

Although automobiles destroyed the carriage industry, they sparked other subsidiary businesses from car repair to gas stations. (NDIRS, 2023.21.8)

In 1921, Swedish immigrant August Johnson, co-owner of Jiffy Manufacturing Company in Fargo, invented a high-pressure grease gun for use on cars, tractors, and other machinery. Learning his trade in a bicycle shop, he started working in garages in 1907 in Devils Lake, North Dakota. Moving to Fargo in 1912, he opened his own shop in 1920 where he developed his grease gun. (NDIRS, Mss 16.1.7)

By the 1920s, Fargoans were also interested in air travel. In 1927, the citizens of the town bought this plane, the "GO-FAR-GO" to compete in the National Air Derby race across the nation. Vernon Roberts flew the plane in the race, but did not make it to the finish line. Coincidentally his propeller flew off while he was passing over Fargo, forcing him to land. (NDIRS, 2023.23.11)

Northwest Airlines started regular service to Fargo in 1931. The planes landed at the new airport, Hector Field, built on land first leased and then given to the city by Martin Hector. (NDIRS, 2070.240.1)

Three

EDUCATION
AND HEALTH

From its earliest days, Fargo took pride in its commitment to education at all levels.

In 1874, the first school in what would become an impressive system was opened—a one-room school at First Avenue and Ninth Street South that served grades one through eight. Other neighborhood schools quickly followed, as did a public high school, opened in 1882.

Dissatisfied with the secularity—or perhaps the evangelical Protestant flavor—of the early public schools, the Presentation Sisters opened the first Catholic school, St. Joseph's Academy, in 1882. Norwegian Lutherans founded the Lutheran Ladies Seminary, which later became Oak Grove High School, in 1906.

Post-secondary education also thrived in Fargo, drawing young people to the city from a wide geographic area. Business schools, barbering and beauty colleges, trade schools, and nurses' training centers sprang up in the city.

Higher education also made an early appearance, with the creation of Fargo College by Congregationalists in 1887 and the opening of the North Dakota Agricultural College in 1891.

Fargo's central location and convenient transportation links also made it a major medical center. Early doctors' offices and sanitaria were supplemented by St. John's Hospital, opened in 1904 as a Catholic establishment, and St. Luke's, a Norwegian Lutheran facility built in 1909. After World War, I the Veteran's Hospital was opened as part of a nationwide effort to provide adequate and convenient health care for veterans of the Great War.

Fargo also became a national leader in public health, working with the Commonwealth Fund to improve the health of mothers and children.

Children play at the Fargo Nursery School, created in 1933 by the Federal Emergency Relief Administration to serve working parents on unemployment relief. The school remained in operation until 1960 when the Lower Front Street neighborhood where it was located was razed for urban renewal. (SHSND, 0075-446-1)

Lincoln School, 617 Fourth Street North, was one of a number of neighborhood schools to which the school board was committed. This building was constructed on the site of the first Lincoln School, which was destroyed in the Great Fire of 1893. It remained in service until 1951. (NDIRS, 2070.287.7)

Students at Woodrow Wilson Elementary School "keeping store" as a classroom exercise. This was eminently practical education for children living in one of America's leading retail centers. (NDIRS, 51.45.3)

The original Fargo Central High School opened in 1882 with an enrollment of 13 boys and 19 girls. The early development of a high school demonstrated the city's commitment to education, a commitment reflected in the startling statistics from the 1930 census that 99 percent of Fargo children aged 7 to 13 were in school and less than one-half of one percent of adult Fargoans were illiterate. (NDIRS, Folio 54.24)

The destruction of "old" Central by a spectacular fire in 1916 was followed by the opening of the "new" Central High in 1921. This school was also lost to a fire in 1966, after which Fargoans decided it was bad luck to name high schools "Central." (NDIRS, 51.10a.1)

The campus of Fargo College was opened south of Island Park by Congregationalists in 1887 as part of an effort to civilize the West. Fargo College offered a liberal arts curriculum, in competition with such regional institutions as Concordia College, Jamestown College, and Wesley College in Grand Forks, and never attracted an enrollment larger than 600. These low enrollments and an anemic endowment doomed the college, which closed in 1922. (David Smith)

The original farmhouse at the North Dakota Agricultural College is pictured above. The NDAC, created under the Morrill Land-Grant College Act of 1862, was built on a section of land about one mile north of Fargo. (NDIRS, Bfa 75)

The first NDAC classes were held in 1891 at Fargo College, while students and faculty waited for the college building to be constructed. "Old Main," as it came to be called, opened for business early in 1892. The building at the far left is Mechanical Arts. (NDIRS, Bol 2)

This photo shows a chemistry class at the NDAC. The college quickly gained a strong reputation in chemistry, polymers, and coatings under the leadership of Edwin Ladd, who became state chemist and, eventually, a United States Senator in 1921. (NDIRS, Dch 35-L 32)

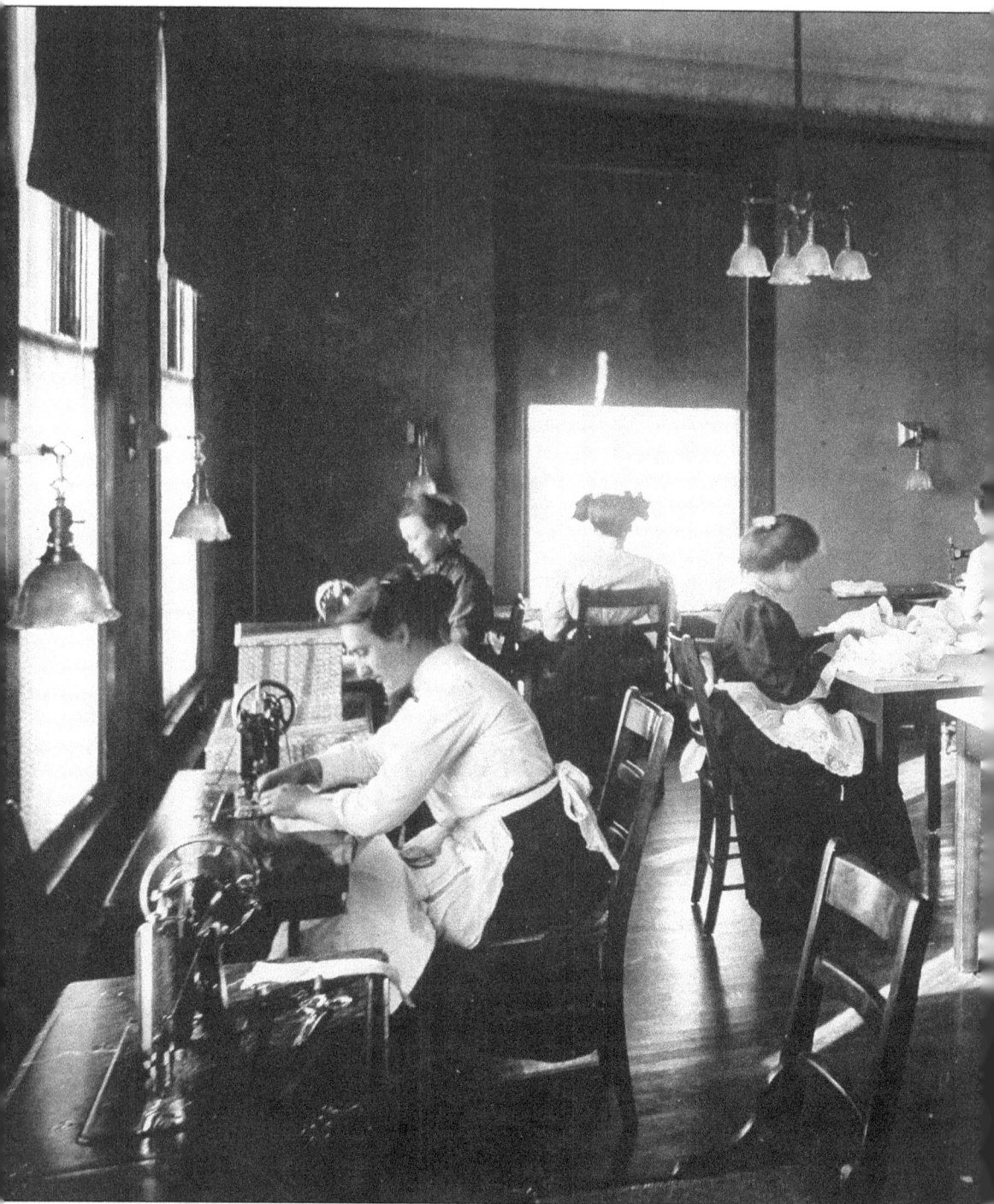

Fargoans lacked enthusiasm for the early NDAC, mainly because they believed it would draw little business to the city. But when the major institutional plums, the penitentiary and the insane asylum, went to Bismarck and Jamestown, respectively, Fargo reluctantly accepted the agricultural college.

The Agricultural College succeeded beyond the expectations of city fathers, drawing students,

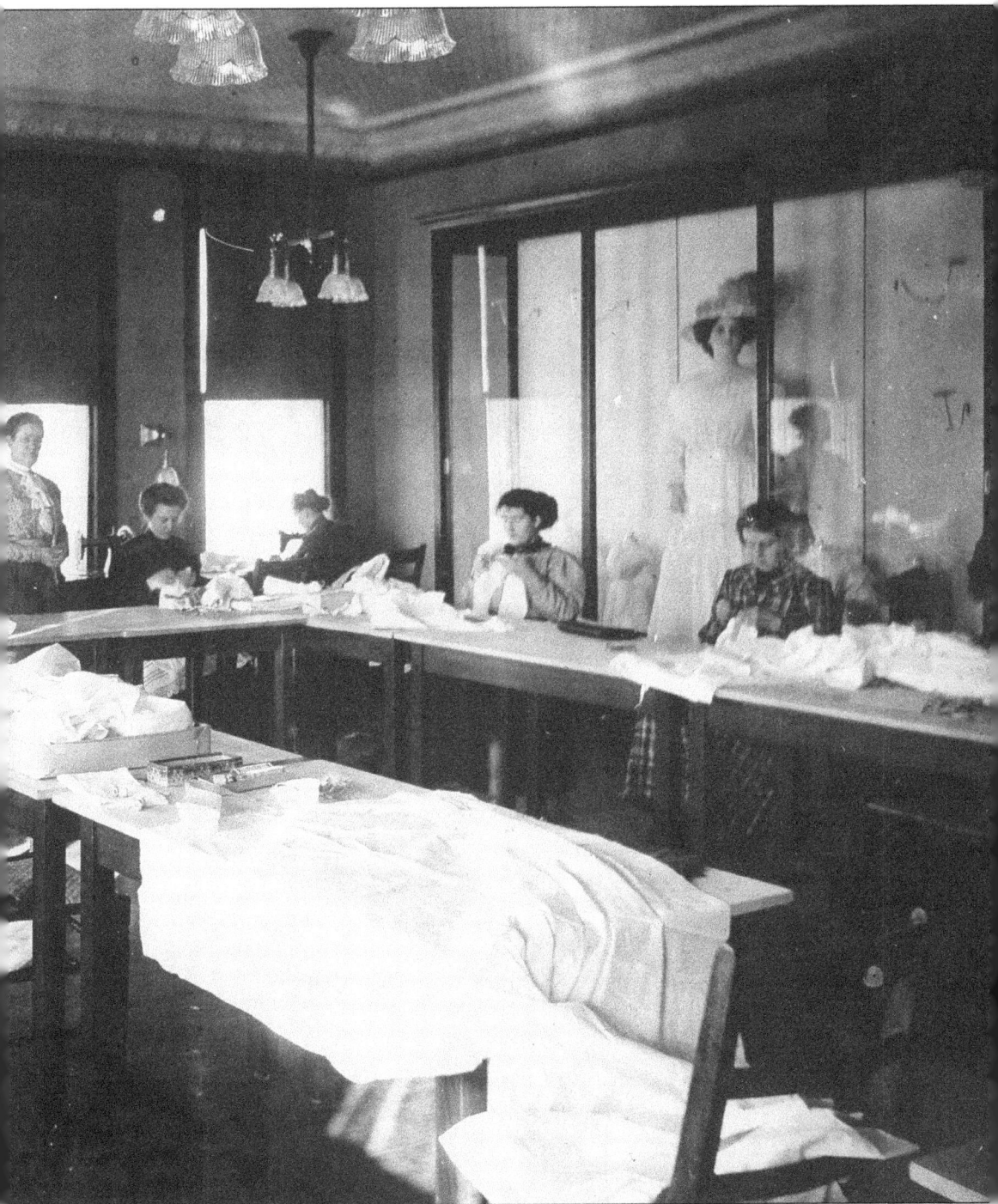

such as these women in a home economics class early in the twentieth century, from all over the region. By 2002, over 10,000 students were attending classes at what had become North Dakota State University, and over 1,900 faculty and staff were employed. Strict gender separation in academics prevailed in fact, if not in law, in the early years, with women concentrated in domestic science and men in engineering and agriculture. (NDIRS, Dho 52-1910)

Football was a mania from the beginning at the NDAC. Here is the 1910 team on the steps of Putnam Hall. (David Smith)

Trade schools and business schools flourished in Fargo. Such institutions as Interstate Business College drew young men and women to Fargo from surrounding communities, and provided them with clerical and business skills that allowed them to move into rapidly expanding white- and pink-collar occupations. (NDIRS, FHC 440-3)

36

These children at Benjamin Franklin Elementary School are applying the common-sense public health lesson that an apple a day keeps the doctor away. (NDIRS, 51.159.1)

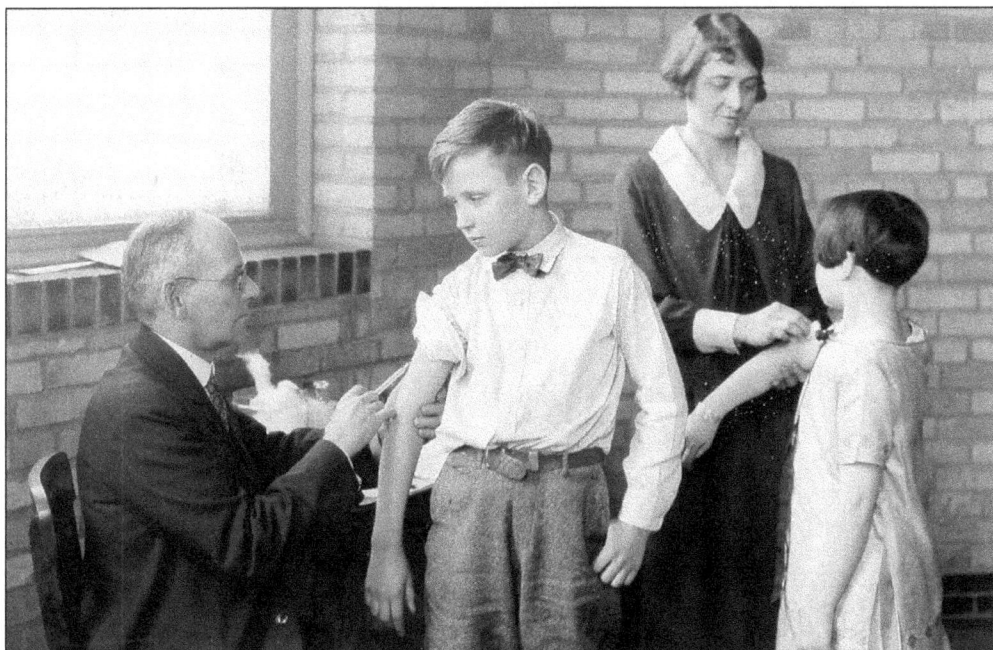

In 1923, the Commonwealth Fund, a national philanthropic organization, initiated a demonstration project to improve Fargoans' health through enhanced pre-natal care and systematic vaccinations for school children. Due in part to this program, by 1930 Fargo was one of the healthiest cities in the country. Here, public health officer B.K. Kilbourne vaccinates a dubious boy for diphtheria. (NDIRS, 51.155.3)

The North Dakota Children's Home, forerunner of Village Family Services, served as a receiving home for infants, an orphanage, an adoption center, and a residence for out-of-town children residing in Fargo for extended medical treatment. (NDIRS, 51.141.1)

Sectarian facilities for children in need also existed in Fargo. St. John's Orphanage was maintained by the Catholic Church. Most orphans lived in such facilities for a year or less. Social workers encouraged adoption, placed children with foster families, and endeavored to reunite neglected children with parents. (David Smith)

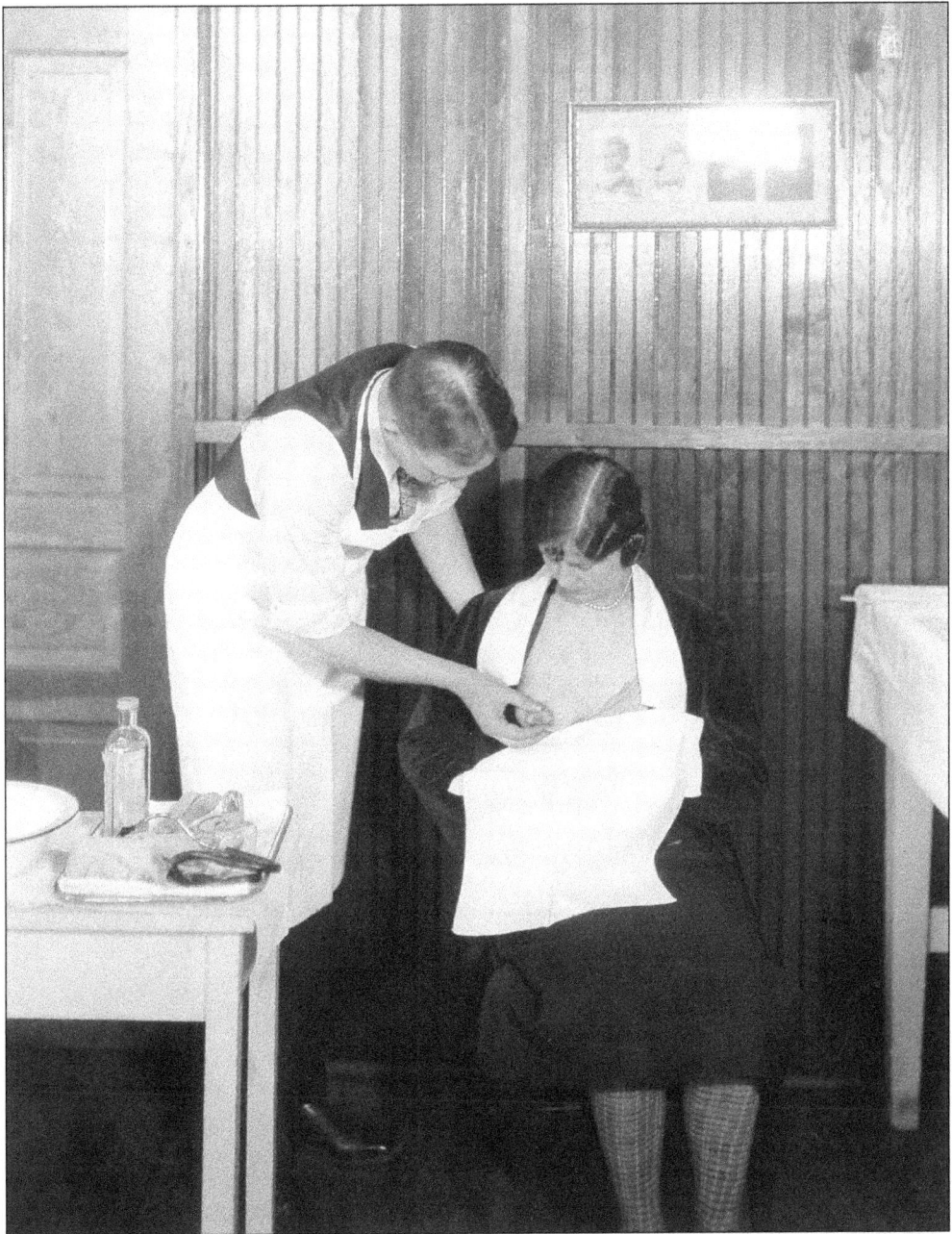

Fargo became a center for a range of medical services just as it became a center for other sorts of services. Early city directories reveal numerous practitioners, orthodox and unorthodox, plying their trade in the Queen City.

Patients needing close attention were frequently housed in physicians' quarters or in sanitaria, but more formal treatment became available in the first decade of the 20th century with the opening of St. John's and St. Luke's Hospitals.

Hospital certification helped guarantee that physicians met certain professional standards, and hospitals also provided formal training for nurses. (NDIRS, 51.151.8)

Fargo's central location made it a logical place for one of the many Veterans' Hospitals constructed after World War I. Fargo's was built along the river, north of the El Zagal bowl. (David Smith)

Fargo maintained the Detention Hospital north of town for the isolation of people suffering from contagious diseases. The building that housed the Detention Hospital is now the home of the Head Start program. (NDIRS, 51.143.1)

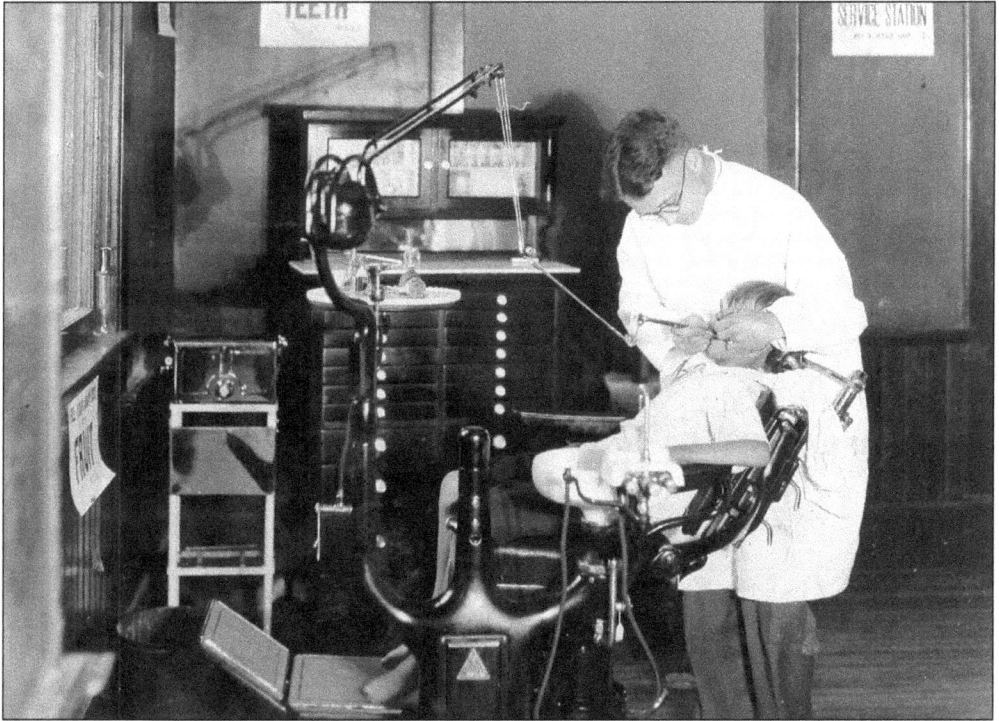

Numerous dentists practiced their profession in Fargo. Increasing public consciousness of the need for good dental health was a major preoccupation of Fargo dentists, along with getting paid for their services! (NDIRS, 51.152.1)

Sanitaria were especially prominent in the days before formal hospital care developed. Sanitaria treated a range of conditions, including physical and mental illnesses, substance abuse, and alcoholism. Treatments were also diverse, ranging from massage therapy to hydrotherapy, with numerous other options in between. (NDIRS, FHC 178-9)

This photo shows Dakota Clinic, just to the northwest of Island Park, in about 1926. The clinic system offered one-stop shopping for patients seeking specialists, who were beginning to replace the general practitioners so abundant in Fargo and elsewhere. The Dakota Clinic building is now part of the MeritCare health system. (NDIRS, 51.144.1)

St. Luke's Hospital was created to meet the health needs of Norwegian Lutherans and was affiliated with the church through its early years. St. Luke's eventually became the basis of MeritCare, which was the largest employer in the city in 2002. (NDIRS, 51.129.13)

Four

AGRICULTURAL CENTER

It is difficult to overstate the significance of agriculture to the early development and subsequent growth of Fargo.

Fargo is centrally located in the Red River Valley of the North, one of the richest agricultural regions of the world. After Oliver Dalrymple and other bonanza farmers demonstrated the possibilities for small grain production in the region with their massive operations of thousands of acres, farmers streamed in from all over the United States and Europe.

Fargo was the most important marketing center in the region, handling millions of bushels of wheat every year and processing numerous agricultural commodities. Much of the early industry in the city revolved around food processing or the manufacture of farm implements.

Fargo was also a major distribution center for implements manufactured elsewhere. Chronically short of labor and draft animals, and farming broad, flat surfaces, Valley farmers were early adopters of agricultural machinery. Tractors, binders, harrows, and cultivators flowed out of Fargo in such prodigious quantities that the city became one of the nation's leaders in implement sales.

Fargo businesses generally survived upon the farm trade. Wholesalers were preoccupied mainly with distributing goods to rural areas, and retailers staged "harvest festivals" and "turkey days" to draw farm families to town.

The State Fair, held in alternate years north of town, was the grandest celebration of the relationship between farm and city, drawing thousands of farm people into town and filling merchants' cash boxes.

Harvest at the Ruliffson farm, west of Fargo, around the turn of the century. Note the number of men and machines the wheat harvest required on large-scale Valley farms. (NDIRS, 2070.128.13)

43

Pictured here is the 1877 harvest at the Cass-Cheney Bonanza, overseen by manager Oliver Dalrymple. Two years later, Dalrymple took 600,000 bushels from 30,000 acres, and President Rutherford B. Hayes came from Washington, D.C. to witness the harvest. (NDIRS, 2029.8.51)

This photo shows threshing on the Cass-Cheney Bonanza. Harvest was the most critical time in the wheat production cycle and, despite increasing mechanization, large-scale producers struggled to secure adequate labor. By World War I, about 30,000 transient farm workers were passing through Fargo every year, mostly at harvest time. (NDIRS, 2070.136.1)

Here farmers' wheat-laden wagons wait to unload at the Union Elevator. Farmers complained bitterly that elevators downgraded their grain unfairly and charged excess dockage, and that the railroads gouged them on rates. Eventually these complaints took institutional form in such radical organizations as the Nonpartisan League. (NDIRS, 2029.8.36)

His elevator full, O.W. Bennett was forced to put 20,000 bushels of wheat on the ground in this 1880 photo. Harvests were usually reliable in the Valley, even during the 1930s when most of the Plains region suffered a devastating drought. (NDIRS, 2029.8.37)

This photo shows penned cattle at the Armour Packing plant in West Fargo, one of the major agricultural processors in the area. During the late 1930s, the village of West Fargo consisted mainly of packinghouse workers, a reality commemorated by the "Packers" team name for West Fargo High School. (NDIRS, 2070.123.5)

Such Fargo firms as Morton & Company carried on a lively trade in farm real estate and loans, most of which they brokered for Eastern investors. The people in the foreground are cigar workers from downstairs. (NDIRS, 51.19.1)

46

Armour Creamery was a major processor of dairy and poultry products, and a major employer of women in Fargo. Agricultural reformers urged wheat farmers to produce cream and eggs as a means of diversifying their incomes. (NDIRS, 2023.95.3)

Minneapolis-Moline was one of many implement manufacturers that maintained distribution facilities in Fargo. Note the tractors with the "streamlining" style, popular in the 1930s. (NDIRS, 2023.30.1)

The North Dakota Agricultural College was a center for agricultural research and education. This is a 1934 photograph of Henry Bolley, longtime NDAC botanist and the discoverer of the cause of "flax wilt," a disease that devastated an important North Dakota crop. (NDIRS, FBo 48.2)

The NDAC encouraged better animal breeding practices by staging contests and offering prizes for animals displaying desirable characteristics. Wheat farmers generally resisted raising livestock, however, because of the work it required. Here a farm boy poses with his prize-winning ewe at the AC. (NDIRS, ExFo 87-I.20)

This machinery was displayed at the North Dakota State Fair in Fargo in about 1930. Fair week was a prime time for implement manufacturers to demonstrate their wares to receptive customers. (NDIRS, 2023.16.1)

The Agricultural Engineering Department at the NDAC was a vigorous advocate of mechanized farming. Here Agricultural Engineering students pose with a steam tractor in front of the college power plant. Note the early harvesting machinery in the background. (NDIRS, ExSt 32.2)

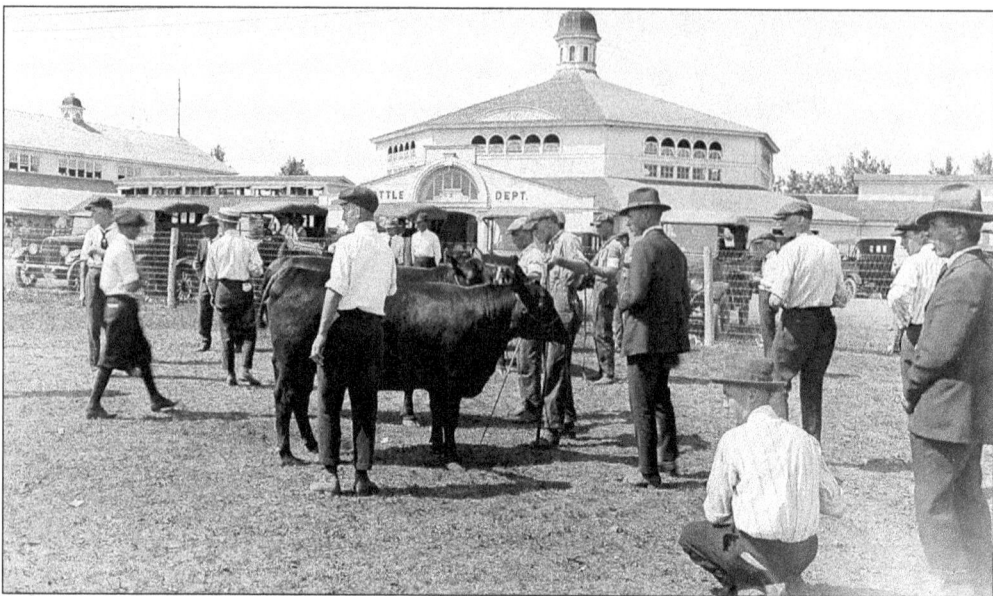

Here cattle are judged at the North Dakota State Fair. The railroads were especially active in encouraging cattle raisers to upgrade their herds. Fargo alternated with Grand Forks in hosting the fair in August. In years when Fargo did not host the State Fair, it put on a smaller, but still impressive, exposition. (NDIRS, 51.48.12)

This grand champion steer was produced by 4-H Club member John McDonald Jr., of Amenia, in 1927. The Powers Hotel purchased the steer and displayed it in the lobby—one of the ways the Fargo business community attempted to promote good relationships with farmers. (NDIRS, 51.38.18)

Five

DISASTERS

Like most other places, Fargo has had its share of disasters, some memorable enough to provide markers in people's lives. Just as Fargoans today vividly remember what they were doing during the flood of 1997, Fargoans a century ago had indelible memories of the Great Fire of 1893.

Some of the city's disasters—such as the 1893 fire—resulted from human action, and the introduction of automobiles and airplanes added a whole new dimension of accidental mishaps. But many disasters that befell the city were natural. Located on the banks of an immature river, Fargoans have faced periodic flooding and sometimes drought. Sharing the continental climate of the Northern Plains, Fargoans have been subject to extremes of heat and cold, as well as to violent weather in the form of winter blizzards, summer cloudbursts, hail storms, and killer tornadoes. Fargoans have a way of accepting difficult weather as a part of life, and even of taking pride in their ability to survive it. As the popular local saying goes, "40 below keeps the riff-raff out."

Some of the natural afflictions visited on people in the area do not rise to the level of disasters, but are certainly annoyances. Clouds of mosquitoes—the unofficial state bird of North Dakota—bedevil Fargoans in wet years, and infestations of grasshoppers and rodents struck the region during the drought of the thirties. Through it all, Fargoans have been well-served by their fatalism and sense of humor.

The Great Fargo Fire of June 7, 1893 began on Front Street—now Main Avenue—when someone carelessly emptied ashes containing live coals into flammable trash. (NDIRS, 51.30.1)

Pushed by a strong south wind, the fire destroyed virtually everything north of Front Street—over one half of the buildings in the city. While police attempted to prevent looting, stunned refugees huddled in tents in Island Park. (NDIRS, 51.30.4)

Miraculously, no lives were lost in the fire, but property loss was devastating. This had been the Stern Block, the Columbia Hotel, and the North Dakota National Bank building. (NDIRS, 50.30.5)

This shows the corner of Second and Broadway after the fire. The fire proved to be a blessing in disguise, because the vigorous rebuilding activity that followed it helped the city avoid the worst effects of the nationwide depression that began in 1893. (NDIRS, 51.30.11)

Even the firehouse, at the corner of NP Avenue and Roberts Street, did not survive the conflagration. Until the World War I years, Fargoans staged a festival every June 7 to celebrate the city's pluck and determination in rebuilding after the fire. (NDIRS, 51.30.14)

Few winters passed without at least one blizzard. In the early days, blizzards would paralyze the city, halting train and streetcar service and confining residents to their homes. (NDIRS, 2070.311.38)

Snow removal was a significant challenge in the days before modern equipment, as well as a major source of winter employment for day laborers. Here, men clear Broadway by hand in front of the Ford Assembly Plant. (NDIRS, 2063.12.7)

Here a streetcar makes its way through a snow canyon during the desperately cold winter of 1936. In January and February of 1936, Fargo's temperature did not rise above zero for nearly three weeks. The streetcars were heated with radiators. (NDIRS, 2063.14.3)

To improve efficiency, men experimented with snow removal using a Caterpillar tractor at the corner of Broadway and First Avenue. (SHSND, 0075-329)

This photo shows Second and Front during the "flood of the century" in 1897. This flood resulted from rapid melting of heavy snow cover. Because the Red River flows north, the lower sections thaw first, and the resulting ice jams exacerbate spring flooding problems. (NDIRS, 2070.226.4)

The Martin Hotel was surrounded by water during the flood. The water levels during the "flood of the century" were reached again in 1997—exactly one hundred years later. (NDIRS, 2065.10.3)

Here, a Fargoan goes to work, or just out to see the sights. This man in a south side neighborhood has decided that a little water won't keep him confined to his home. (NDIRS, 51.32b.7)

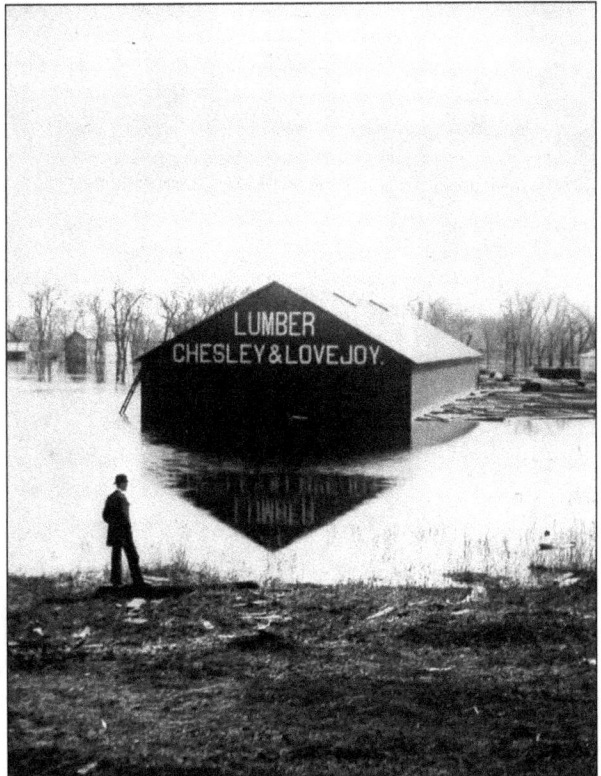

The 1897 flood was spectacular, but it was hardly the only event of its kind. Spring thaws and summer cloudbursts frequently raised the Red above its banks, as this 1881 view of the riverfront in the spring demonstrates. (NDIRS, 2029.8.34)

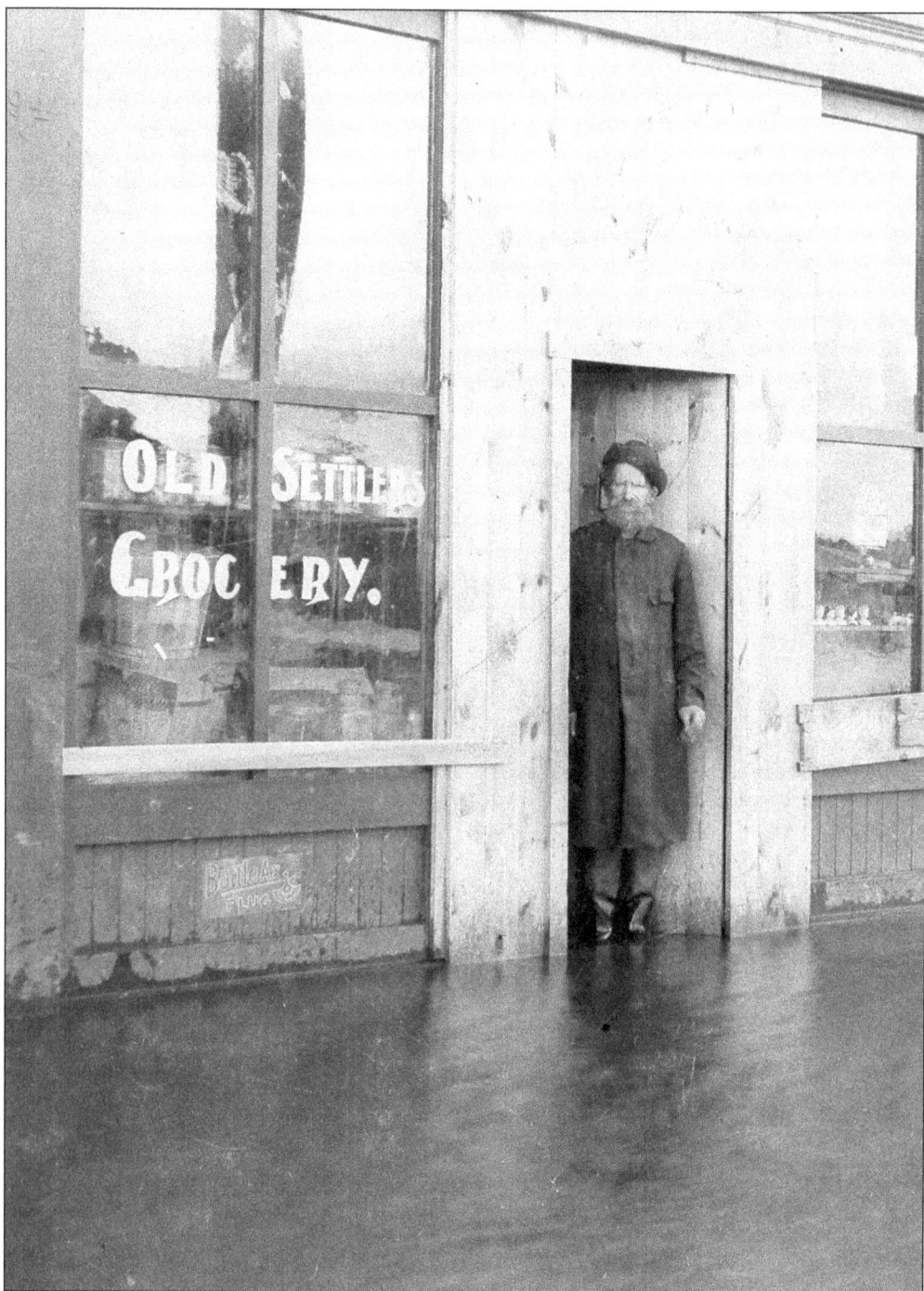

This "old settler" is ready to provide service, but not with a smile. In the early years, Fargoans accepted periodic flooding as a part of life, but by the 1960s they were undertaking substantial diking and river re-channelization to attempt to control their capricious river. (NDIRS, 2065.10.5)

Two south side ladies inspect what has suddenly become lakefront property during the flood of 1897. (NDIRS, 2042.10.2)

The Fargo equivalent of a gondolier moves along First Avenue South. During the flood of 1897, Fargoans employed Venetian modes of transportation but did not duplicate the charms of Italian living. (NDIRS, 2065.15.2)

It was feast or famine on the Red, as this picture from 1910 illustrates. In drought years, the river stopped flowing and residents could walk across its bed. During the drought of the 1930s, the river stopped flowing nearly every year—for over 200 days in 1936. (NDIRS, 328.2.18)

Dry years brought rodent infestations to the region, or perhaps they just made the depredations of the existing rodent population more noticeable. Here is a pile of flickertail gophers killed by poisoned oats. (NDIRS, ExGo 63.5)

Grasshoppers thrive under dry conditions, and were especially devastating during the 1930s. Here men mix grasshopper bait—bran, molasses, and arsenic—which will be spread on fields to kill hoppers. An unanticipated consequence of this activity was the leaching of arsenic into the ground water in many North Dakota communities. (NDIRS, ExGr 37)

This is the Plymouth Congregational Church, destroyed by a tornado that struck the city in the early morning hours of July 7, 1890. This storm claimed the lives of seven children, all in one family. (NDIRS, 2065.29.2)

A Northern Pacific passenger train was knocked off the tracks by the killer tornado of 1890. Several passengers were injured, but there were no fatalities. The water in the background is Long Lake, a large slough west of the NDAC that was drained in the 1920s. (NDIRS, 2065.29.1)

Introduction of the automobile multiplied the number of accidents human beings could cause. This driver on NP Avenue lost control of his car—or perhaps he was just in a hurry to get to Interstate Investment Company. (NDIRS, 2070.337.1)

Grocery stores delivered in Fargo prior to World War II, but the customers of Baldwin Market were going to have to wait because the driver managed to find a tree. (NDIRS, 2070.336.23)

The chemistry laboratory at the NDAC exploded and burned on Christmas Eve of 1909. There were no fatalities because school was out for the holiday, and even the hyperactive chemist Edwin Ladd took Christmas Eve off to be with his family. (NDIRS, Bch 35)

This airplane crashed in the NDAC pasture in July of 1920. Like many Americans, Fargoans were fascinated with flying machines and flying. They were less enamored with crashing. (NDIRS, Aca 54-III.4)

Six

RELIGION AND CULTURE

Religion has played a significant role in the life of the city ever since the first church services were held in a tent at "Fargo on the Prairie."

By 1930, the city claimed to be home to more churches per capita than any other city in the United States, and over 70 percent of Fargoans were reckoned to be church members. The religiosity of the city, and the state, was underpinned by statewide prohibition and by restrictive blue laws that forbade dances and the exhibition of movies on Sundays, and mandated that most retail establishments be closed for the Sabbath.

Churches were more than just religious institutions. They were also social and recreational centers and vehicles for cultural expression and the preservation of ethnic distinctions. The large Norwegian population of Fargo meant that Lutheranism was the dominant religious persuasion, but there was a significant Catholic presence, especially among residents of German and Irish background. The Yankees, who were disproportionately represented in business and the professions, and the Canadian Scots were found mainly in the Presbyterian, Methodist, Congregational, Episcopalian, and Baptist churches. And the Jewish community was substantial enough to support a thriving synagogue.

Churches, important as they were, were not the only centers of culture in the city. An impressive array of fraternal and patriotic organizations, singing societies, women's clubs, and dancing and card clubs enlivened life in the city, cemented social bonds, and undertook a variety of philanthropic endeavors.

The Sunday School class of Plymouth Congregational Church poses in May of 1924. (NDIRS, 51.177.2)

St. Mary's Cathedral has had the distinction of being Fargo's most elegant church since its completion in 1899. Built by prominent Catholic layman James Kennedy, St. Mary's is headquarters of the Fargo diocese of the Catholic Church. One of the first Western Cardinals, Aloisius Muench, was Bishop of Fargo in the 1930s and 1940s. (NDIRS 51. 11.9)

North Dakota has always had a higher percentage of Roman Catholics than the national average. Fargo Catholics sought education as well as spiritual care. Sacred Heart Academy, on North Broadway, served as the first Catholic high school in the city. (David Smith)

First Lutheran had its origins in a Norwegian Lutheran congregation formed in 1874. This handsome edifice, built across the street from St. Mary's, hosted its first service on Christmas Day of 1919. First Lutheran was the largest Lutheran church in the city, claiming a membership of nearly 2,500 by the 1930s. (SHSND, 0075-571)

Gethsemane Episcopal Church in south Fargo counted many prominent business and professional people among its members. (SHSND, c3697)

Fargo's Jewish population was served by this synagogue across from Island Park on First Avenue South. Early Fargo had a substantial Jewish population, concentrated in the Lower Front Street area where this synagogue was located. Banker Alex Stern was the most prominent Jew in the city, but Jews were also significant in real estate, retailing, and in the grain trade. Along with Catholics, Jews received negative attention during the 1920s from Fargo's Ku Klux Klan. (NDIRS, 424.1.3)

Pontoppidan Lutheran, founded in 1877, was one of several Norwegian Lutheran congregations in the city. Services in most of the churches were performed in Norwegian exclusively until World War I, when pressure from Americanizers forced them to add services in English. Most had dropped their Norwegian services entirely by the 1940s. (NDIRS, 2049.48.2)

The rich musical tradition fostered by the Catholic and Lutheran churches enjoyed vibrant secular manifestations. Here Valley City native Peggy Lee entertains a group in a home. Early in her professional career Lee moved to Fargo and performed at the Powers Hotel. (NDIRS, P129.3)

THE AMPHION MALE CHORUS
NORTH DAKOTA STATE DAY
A CENTURY OF PROGRESS
AUGUST 30 1933

CHICAGO
1933
KAUFMANN+FABRY
OFFICIAL PHOTOGRAPHERS

The Amphion Male Chorus was a Fargo-Moorhead ensemble that performed at the 1933 World's Fair in Chicago, went on several Eastern tours, and was featured on national network radio programs. The chorus was the source of great pride in the community, which conducted impressive fund-raising campaigns to make its travels possible. (NDIRS, 51.191.1)

This photo shows students at Fargo College circling a maypole. The colleges were major sources for cultural enrichment in the city, bringing performers and speakers from all over the country for public programs. The colleges also staged plays and concerts that enlivened the cultural scene, while their students and faculty raised Fargo's intellectual tone. (NDIRS, Mss 153.3.9)

Festival Concert Hall, at the NDAC, hosted numerous concerts and lectures to which the public was invited. Built in 1897 as an armory, Festival Hall was used for classes, athletic events, public programs, and even political conventions. It was demolished in 1982. (NDIRS, BFe 77-042.10)

The Fargo Public Library was a gift to the city from steelmaker Andrew Carnegie in 1903. Of the three Carnegie libraries that once graced the city, only one—Putnam Hall at NDSU—still stands. (NDIRS, 2070.277.1)

The Young Men's Christian Association was a major religious and recreational organization in the city. Organized in 1886, it moved into this structure in 1907. Fargo also had an active YWCA that provided recreation, religious guidance, and a residential facility for young women and girls. (SHSND, 0132-19)

A college YMCA was built across the street from the main gate of the NDAC to serve the needs of students. This building was destroyed by a tornado that struck the north side in 1957. (NDIRS, 2042.4.7)

The Grand Army of the Republic was a major patriotic organization in Fargo, as it was in most communities where significant numbers of Union veterans lived. This parade took place during the State Encampment of the GAR, held in Fargo in June of 1892. (NDIRS, 2042.25.13)

In 1916, the GAR erected this statue of a common soldier in honor of their fallen comrades from the Civil War. The monument still stands at the foot of Broadway in Island Park. (SHSND, 0135-17)

The Masonic Temple was decked out in patriotic bunting for this picture, taken about 1915. Built in 1899, the Temple housed meeting rooms, offices, a lending library, a ballroom, and recreational facilities. Fraternal organizations like the Masons played a major role in Fargo. (David Smith)

Another significant fraternal organization was the Elks, whose lodge is pictured here. Membership in fraternal organizations and service clubs allowed Fargoans to serve the community in systematic way, provided a range of recreational opportunities for their families, and facilitated the creation and maintenance of valuable business contacts. (NDIRS, FHC 624-1)

74

The Norwegian cultural heritage was much in evidence in early Fargo. This statue of Henrick Wergeland, Norwegian poet and champion of the Jews, was given to the people of Fargo by Norway. It still stands in the center of Island Park. (SHSND, A5949)

Norwegian Crown Prince Olav and Crown Princess Marthe acknowledged Fargo's Norse heritage during a 1939 visit. Here some of the royal party leaves Louis Hanna's elegant home on South Eighth Street. Former Governor Hanna hosted the royal couple during their visit to the city. (NDIRS, 2023.60.15)

This photo shows the dedication of the statue of Rollo near the Great Northern depot during the Sangerfest celebration in 1912. Rollo was the Viking who became the first Duke of Normandy in 911 A.D.—thus the French flag on the left—and his descendant, William the Conqueror, seized the English throne in 1066. Two thousand people turned out for the dedication and the celebration of Fargo's Norwegian heritage. The Rollo statue now stands in a small park of its own, across from the Sons of Norway Hall, appropriately enough. (NDIRS, 51.50.7)

Seven

WORK AND BUSINESS

From its earliest days, when the rowdy folks in "Fargo in the Timber" opened saloons and brothels, Fargo has meant business.

Especially in its early years, Fargo business was fueled by the growth of the city itself. Lumber yards, building contractors, realtors, and bankers enjoyed remarkable financial success, while helping to provide the infrastructure for the Gateway City. Manufacturers also made an early appearance, especially food processors and other enterprisers that targeted the local market.

But Fargo's central location and its superior competitive rail connections decreed that its greatest economic strength would be in the wholesaling and retailing of goods produced elsewhere. Wholesalers built warehouses and distribution centers, and traveling salesmen fanned out to the northwest from their Fargo base. Fargo's numerous retail stores attracted rural customers with their competitive prices, imaginative promotions, and sophisticated styles. By the early twentieth century, Fargo was consistently among the nation's leaders in retail sales per capita.

Fargo attracted more than customers. The attractive business climate drew national chains, such as Sears and Red Owl, to town. And the vibrant employment market drew workers, especially from surrounding rural areas. Particularly noteworthy was the number of young women who came to Fargo to fill the numerous clerical and retail jobs the city offered, and to make new lives for themselves.

The lumber business was big business in early Fargo, as this 1880 photograph of the Crockett and Shotwell Yards indicates. A number of Fargo fortunes were built on lumber and real estate. (NDIRS, 2029.8.28)

This photo shows mill hands at the Schlanser and Ostbye woodworking shop in 1899. John Schlanser came to the city as a Swiss-immigrant carpenter in 1879 and grew wealthy by tying his fortunes to Fargo's growth. By the time he died in 1932, Schlanser was a revered lay leader in the Catholic Church and a dependable mover behind civic causes. (NDIRS, 51.54.2)

Here a work crew lays sidewalk along North Broadway in the 1920s. City government faced a continual challenge in keeping up with Fargo's growth. (NDIRS, 51.46.1)

A growing city needed a communications infrastructure as well as sidewalks and water mains, and the telephone company provided it. Prior to World War I, the telephone was mainly a device for business communication in Fargo, but during the 1920s residential service expanded dramatically. (NDIRS, 2023.83.3)

The steam plant of the Northern States Power Company provided the steam heat to downtown businesses through underground tunnels until 1960. Electric service in Fargo began in 1881. In 1910 the Union Power and Light Company was acquired by Northern States Power, now Xcel Energy. (NDIRS, 2063.6.10)

SET NO. 9   10/15/29
NORTHERN STATES POWER Co.
ENGINEERING CONTRACT NO. 2965
BOILER PLANT EXTENSION - FARGO STEAM PLANT
NEW STACKS - FINAL

Fargo's location and its rapid growth made it a regional banking center. Fargo banks, such as the First National Bank pictured here, enjoyed a reputation for conservatism and fiduciary responsibility that was rare for banks in rapidly growing areas. (NDIRS, 51.4.7)

Martin Hector came to Fargo without capital in 1872, but by 1897 he was comfortable enough to become one of the founders and the first president of Fargo National Bank. Among the other Fargoans who built at least part of their fortunes in banking were Louis B. Hanna, Alex Stern, E.J. Weiser, and Fred Irish. (NDIRS, P101.2)

Loungers stand in front of the Merchants State Bank, an edifice whose grandeur is somewhat diminished by the dirt thoroughfares. State reserve requirements were low and state oversight was lax, contributing to the creation of more banks than were necessary. By 1920 there were nearly 900 banks in North Dakota. (NDIRS, 51.4.1)

This shot shows officers and employees of the Merchants State Bank. The relative soundness and probity of Fargo banks was illustrated by the fact that none failed during the Great Depression of the 1930s. (NDIRS, 51.4.3)

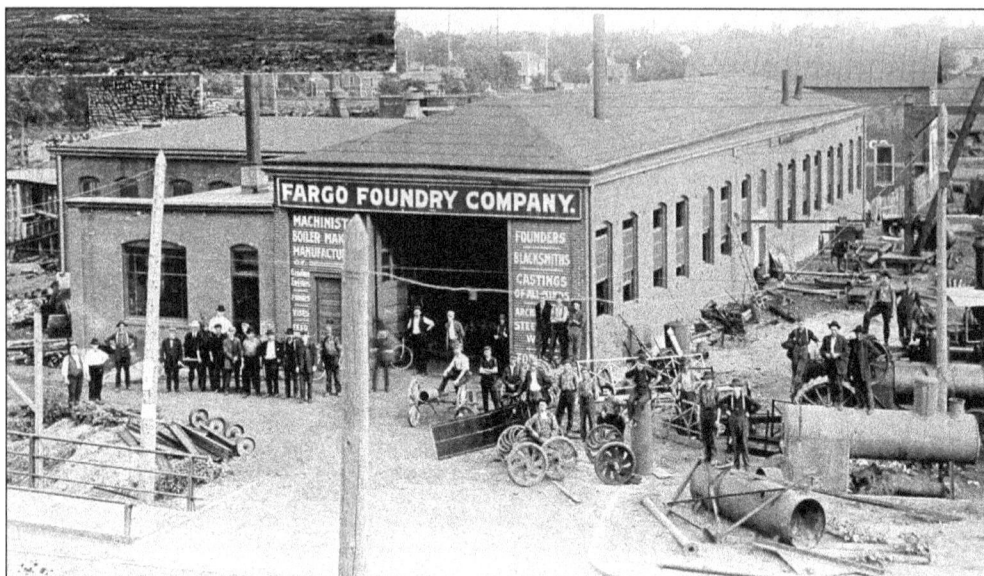

The Fargo Foundry, a metal fabricator, was one of the largest industrial employers in early Fargo. The bulk, weight, and relatively low value of its products gave it an effective monopoly on local markets. The Fargo Foundry, one of the city's oldest businesses, continues to operate. (NDIRS, Mss 1970.46.1)

Another large industrial employer in early Fargo was Everhart Candy (later Chaney-Everhart) pictured here shortly after the turn of the century. Founded by C.A. Everhart in 1895, the company discontinued operations in 1932. (NDIRS, 2042.9.3)

The difficulties of keeping cigars fresh dictated that most were manufactured for local consumption prior to World War I. Here are hand rollers working at the Sulzbach Cigar Factory in 1909. (NDIRS, 51.19.2)

Members of the Leather Workers Union posed for this picture, probably in the mid-1910s. While many construction workers, machinists, and newspaper workers were unionized, Fargo employers were generally hostile to collective bargaining. An employer lockout in 1913–1914 devastated the building trades unions, and vigilante action in 1935 helped break a coal-drivers' strike. (David Smith)

The abundance of clerical, retail, and personal service jobs available in Fargo attracted numerous single young women to the city. These secretaries are working at the W. J. Lane Company, a realtor and insurance broker, nine years after the firm opened in 1902. (NDIRS, 2042.32.18)

Single women who could afford to do so embraced apartment living in such buildings as the Ramona Apartments on North Broadway. Apartments have been a prominent feature in Fargo housing since its early days. Women with fewer resources lived in boarding houses or in rooms provided by the YWCA and other philanthropic organizations. (NDIRS, FHC 311-2)

Numerous personal service jobs were available in Fargo to women who lacked the training for office work. Here two waitresses pose at the Dutch Maid Ice Cream Store, probably about 1940. The Dutch Maid was opened in the mid-thirties by Ralph Brandmeyer and Allen Crawford and quickly became a popular rendezvous for teenagers. (NDIRS, 2023.L-1)

The Elliott House was built by former steamboat hand Peter Elliott in 1882 and quickly became a popular local hostelry. Note the sizeable staff that has been assembled for this mid-1880s photograph. (NDIRS, 2070.504.5)

The Gardner, pictured here about 1938, became one of Fargo's leading downtown hotels following its opening in 1909. One of the keys to its success was its favorable location, right across the street from the Federal Courthouse. (NDIRS, 2023.88.8)

Note the informality and implied conviviality of the Elliott House lobby, pictured here in the mid-1880s. Proprietor Elliott is leaning on the counter, and his wife and son are the people dressed in black in the center of the picture. (NDIRS, 2070.504.1)

The lobby of the Gardner, by contrast, appears cold, formal, and antiseptic. Note how the clerks are separated from customers by bars and granite similar to the separation of bank tellers from their customers. (NDIRS, 2023.L-38)

The A. C. Grocery was located just across the street from the main gate of the NDAC. Fargo was a city of tiny groceries. By the early 1930s there were nearly 100 of them, or one for every 300 residents. (NDIRS, FHC 1-1)

By the late thirties national or regional chains such as Red Owl were offering stiff competition to neighborhood groceries. "Cash and carry" stores did not extend credit or deliver groceries as the mom-and-pops did, but they compensated with substantially lower prices. (NDIRS, 2023.91.2)

Laundries, such as the Model Laundry on NP Avenue, pictured here in the late twenties, were important Fargo businesses. They appealed to customers on the grounds of convenience—they picked up and delivered—and on the grounds of safety. Fargoans' attempts to dry clean their own clothes with gasoline and other flammables caused many serious accidents. (NDIRS, Mss 34.1.2)

New businesses continually developed to serve modern needs and tastes. The Johnson Cycle Supply House expanded from bicycles to motorcycles in the early twentieth century. They also sold firearms to their customers. (NDIRS, 51.181.4)

Bergstrom and Crowe was one of several large furniture retailers in Fargo. Founded in 1908 by J.B. Bergstrom and George W. Crowe, it thrived by serving the furniture needs of the rapidly growing city and the surrounding rural areas. (NDIRS, 2070.160.1)

The Herbst Department Store, opened by Isaac Herbst in 1891, was one of the leading retailers in the city, along with DeLendrecie's, Moody's, and several others. The Herbst family—especially Isaac's wife, Emma—was renowned for its paternalistic concern for employees and philanthropic generosity to the community. (NDIRS, 2043.5.22)

Longtime druggist Lars Christianson mixes a concoction in his Front Street store in 1896. A Norwegian immigrant, Christianson bought his store in 1881 and managed it actively for over 50 years. (NDIRS, 51.27.2)

Small-scale druggists such as Christianson, second from the left in this 1886 photograph, were numerous in Fargo in the early days of the city. In addition to meeting Fargoans' pharmaceutical needs, they also had the reputation of providing under-the-counter liquor to trusted customers. (NDIRS, 51.27.3)

Warehousing was an important enterprise in Fargo, which was a major wholesale and distribution center. The Fargo Food Products Company, located on the Great Northern tracks, distributed canned and boxed foods in the Northern Plains region. (NDIRS, FHC 370-6)

Sears and other chains sometimes partnered with local retailers such as George Black when entering a new area. Black was prohibited from attaching his name to a new enterprise when he dissolved his partnership with Sears in 1934, so he shrewdly called the shop he opened nearby the "Store Without a Name." The Black Building was the tallest building in the state for a few months in 1930–1931, until it was surpassed by the new state capitol.(David Smith)

Eight

LIVING WITH THE RIVER

Fargo's relationship with the Red River has always been ambivalent. The river has been a lifeline and a threat, a recreational resource and a dumping ground, a connector and a divider.

In the city's early years the river was an avenue of commerce, connecting Fargo to Winnipeg and points in between. The river was a source of water and finding adequate water and making it potable was a challenge from the beginning. But the river was also a place where garbage and debris was dumped and raw sewage was emptied, and transients who were not welcomed in the neighborhoods clustered along its banks.

The river could be a threat. Swimmers, boaters, and people crossing the ice lost lives with appalling regularity, and floods threatened the entire community. Eventually, managing the river and enhancing its safety became priorities.

Bridging the river and connecting the cities of Fargo and Moorhead was another priority. And while the river did not present a major engineering problem to bridge-builders, it was politically complicated to build bridges between two different cities, counties, and states.

The river was always a recreational resource, but Fargoans eventually came to perceive it as a potential garden spot and began the process of transforming it from an eyesore to a stream whose natural beauty would draw and hold visitors.

This scene of the riverfront in 1879 illustrates what a busy commercial corridor the Red was in Fargo's early history. The extension of the Great Northern to the north diminished and eventually doomed commercial river traffic. (NDIRS, 328.2.1)

The river could threaten commerce as well, as it did during the flood of 1897. The Northern Pacific parked locomotives and loaded freight cars on its bridge, reasoning that they would stabilize it and prevent it from being carried away. (NDIRS, 328.2.4)

In drought years, the river was not an avenue of commerce or much of anything else. Note the bleak aspect of the riverfront and the piles of garbage and debris in the foreground. Much of the debris from the Great Fire was dumped along the riverbank. (NDIRS, 328.2.17)

This is Fargo's city waterworks at the turn of the century. Providing water of adequate volume and purity has been a concern in Fargo since the city's beginning. Note the footbridge to Moorhead on the right. (NDIRS, 51.140.2)

The Fargo sewage disposal plant was built in the 1930s with help from the federal Public Works Administration. Prior to the opening of this plant, Fargo—along with Moorhead—dumped its raw sewage into the Red in the downtown area. As the community grew, this method of sewage disposal aroused aesthetic and health concerns, especially in years of low river flow. (NDIRS, 2023.L-145)

Fargo workmen dismantle the footbridge in March of 1922 to protect it from damage from flowing ice. Ice companies harvested ice from the Red to cool iceboxes. River ice was substantially cheaper than ice harvested from Minnesota lakes, an indication of the Red's poor reputation for cleanliness. (NDIRS, 2022.5.2)

The growing popularity of automobiles increased pressures for more and better bridges between Fargo and Moorhead, but political disputes between jurisdictions made construction a difficult proposition. (NDIRS, 2023.2.3)

Steamboats and grain boats are gathered near the Grandin Elevator in this early photograph. The extension of railroads to the north and the problem of flooding led elevator operators to abandon the riverfront by 1900. (NDIRS, 51.51.15)

During the 1930s, the city made a sustained effort to clean up and beautify the riverfront, usually by utilizing the labor of the unemployed. Here is a Works Progress Administration crew about to go to work on a river improvement project.(NDIRS, 2065.35.1)

This photograph from about 1910 shows a group of Fargo and Moorhead residents enjoying a spring day by fishing in and strolling along the Red near the South Dam. The city dammed the river to assure adequate water supplies. (NDIRS, 51.138.11)

This 1926 photograph shows boys shooting a rifle into the river, perhaps at some luckless beaver or muskrat they have spotted. Discharging of firearms in the city parks and along the river was a matter of substantial concern among police and homeowners during the 1920s and 1930s. (NDIRS, 51.138.7)

This boy was enjoying a summer day at the "ol' swimmin' hole," maintained by the Park Board above the South Dam. The footbridge between Fargo and Moorhead can be seen stretching across the picture. Nearby was Dommer's Boathouse, a major Moorhead landmark that rented canoes. (David Smith)

The Roanoke was one of several small boathouses that rented canoes to people hoping to enjoy the river. Beautification of the riverfront, removal of snags, and the development of sewage disposal facilities made the Red a much more attractive recreational venue. (SHSND, A5932)

These children are enjoying the river at the South Dam. The Park Board banned swimming when the river stopped flowing over the dam in order to protect public health. These restrictions became so onerous in the thirties that the city decided to build the Island Park Pool as an alternative to river swimming. (NDIRS, 2023.12.1)

Nine

POLITICS
AND GOVERNMENT

As a small city in a distant and sparsely populated region, Fargo did not play a significant role in national politics. Still, there was the occasional Presidential visitor, first Rutherford B. Hayes in 1879 and most recently George W. Bush in 2001. In addition, Fargo got caught up in such major national events as entry into World War I and the crisis of the Great Depression.

Within the state of North Dakota, Fargo was the largest city, but it was out of step politically with much of the state. A bastion of conservatism in a state characterized by agrarian radicalism, Fargo resisted the Equity Society, the Nonpartisan League, the Farmers Holiday Association, and other expressions of agricultural pain and anger. Fargo's conservatism and its relative prosperity earned for it the enmity of much of the rest of the state, which referred derisively to its county as "Imperial Cass."

Local government was usually more significant to Fargoans than the state or federal governments. It was local government that levied the taxes that fell most heavily on people prior to World War II. And it was local government that used the revenues raised to do most of the things people needed to have government do—build the roads and sidewalks, protect persons and property, provide water and dispose of sewage, build and run schools, and maintain parks. Fargo prided itself on doing these necessary things cheaply and efficiently.

Theodore Roosevelt speaks to a Fargo crowd during a whistle stop campaign tour. A great favorite with voters generally, Roosevelt was especially beloved by North Dakotans because of his ranching adventure in the Little Missouri country in the 1880s. (NDIRS, 0410-173)

101

Fargo boys march west on Front Street, now Main Avenue, on their way to whip the Kaiser. Fargoans were enthusiastic supporters of the Allied cause during World War I. Seven thousand people—one-third of the city—turned out in a driving rainstorm for one patriotic rally. (NDIRS, 2042.25.1)

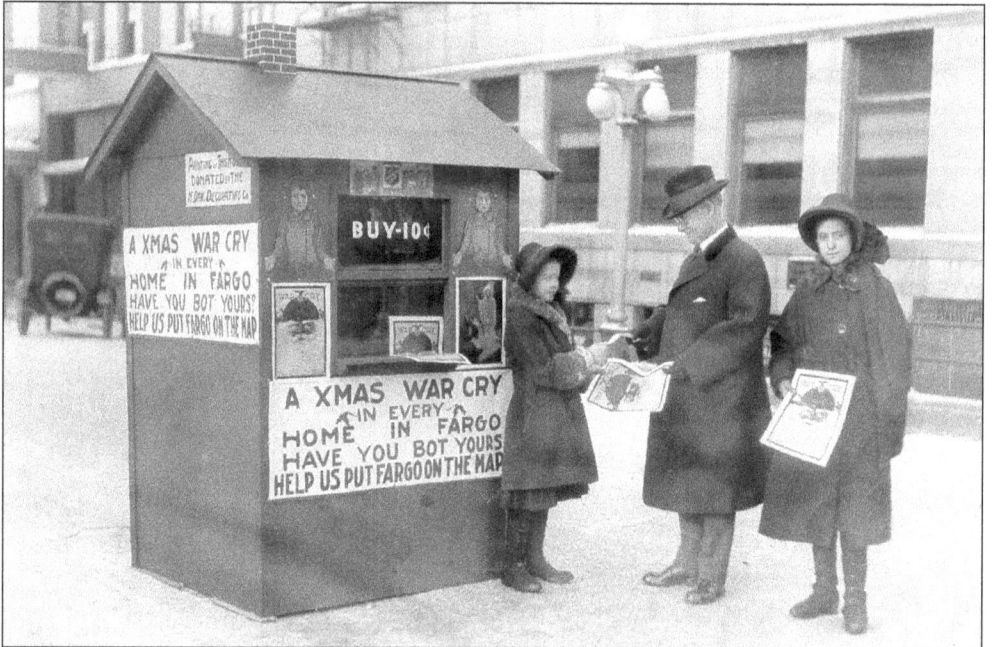

Fundraisers receive a wartime donation from prominent Fargoan H. W. Gearey, later mayor of the city. Residents oversubscribed Liberty Loan campaigns and contributed generously to the Red Cross and other agencies, but at times their patriotism took an ugly turn, as when they forced closure of the Unitarian Church because of the pacifism of its minister, William Ballou. (NDIRS, 51.176.1)

102

Fargo's first postmaster was Gordon J. Keeney, who set up shop in a grocery store in 1873. Postmasters were political appointees, and the local party lusted after these jobs. (NDIRS, Mss 1970.5.4)

Fargo's growth led to a more impressive federal presence. The first federal building, pictured above, was designed by the renowned Hancock Brothers architectural firm in the 1890s and housed the post office and the federal court. (NDIRS, 51.43.5)

The growing significance of the federal government in people's lives and its expanding functions meant that it quickly outgrew its Fargo quarters. By 1930 a new federal building was going up on First and Roberts. (NDIRS, 2023.32.5)

The completed federal building, which quickly became a Fargo landmark, eventually proved inadequate. In 1970, the post office and other federal offices were separated from the courts and moved to a new building, and in 1998 the court was essentially doubled in size with the addition of the Quentin N. Burdick Courthouse to the west of the existing building. (NDIRS, 2042.26.2)

The personification of Fargo conservatism was Louis B. Hanna, the millionaire lumber dealer, banker, and real estate speculator who served as governor between 1912 and 1916. Hanna's cavalier dismissal of farmers' concerns helped fuel anger that resulted in creation of the Nonpartisan League. (NDIRS, 2070.408.1)

Elizabeth Preston Anderson was the longtime president of the state Women's Christian Temperance Union and a crusader for moral purity in Fargo and the state of North Dakota. In addition to campaigning against liquor, prostitution, permissive divorce laws, and other moral evils, Preston and the WCTU also worked for woman's suffrage. (NDIRS, P4.2)

Fargo's City Hall, which also included the fire station, police station, and jail, was built at the corner of NP and Roberts in 1910. Considered woefully inadequate by 1930, it continued to house most of city government until the present facility opened in 1961. (NDIRS, 51.26.12)

This Cass County Courthouse was built in 1906 after a fire destroyed its predecessor. Joined to the stately red sandstone structure on the other side was the county jail and sheriff's residence. (NDIRS, 51.9.5)

The Fargo Police Department poses with bicycles in front of the post office in this 1898 photograph. This image of modernity is somewhat misleading, because most early officers walked beats. (NDIRS, 2070.275.1)

The advent of the automobile allowed—and to a large degree compelled—the Fargo police to become more mobile. The growing tendency of miscreant motorists to ignore beat cops' shouts of "stop" in the early 1930s led a frustrated department to purchase motorcycles and eventually "prowl" cars, in which radios were installed in 1935. Still, as late as 1940, downtown was patrolled mainly by policemen on foot. (NDIRS, 51.42.3)

The "smoke eaters" of Engine Company One are pictured here in the 1890s. In Fargo, as in many cities, the firemen were the most admired public employees and were kept busy in a town with lots of wooden structures, cast iron stoves, and kerosene lamps. The firemen were especially revered for their heroic, but futile, efforts to stop the Great Fire of 1893. No wonder so many little boys wanted to grow up to be one of these men. (NDIRS, 2070.215.4)

Ten

RECREATION

As a regional hub, Fargo developed as a center for recreation. Using almost any excuse to celebrate, the residents turned out as often as possible for parades, galas, and famous visitors. In addition to these municipality-wide events, Fargoans also enjoyed recreation centered around the city's many educational facilities, including high school sports, college theater, and homecoming celebrations.

Despite challenging weather, or perhaps because of it, Fargoans have always made a point of playing outside as much as possible. From the early days of the city, when good hunting was still possible in Fargo, to the mid-twentieth century when golf courses proliferated, the city's people have had a long history of making their own amusement outdoors. The city government also concerned itself with beautification and recreation, expanding on the Northern Pacific Railroad's gift of land for Island Park to create a multi-park system by 1900.

In addition to outdoor pursuits, Fargo developed an active entertainment culture indoors. From dance halls to theaters and later movie houses, middle-class Fargoans had a wide choice of venues. For the less law-abiding, illegal entertainment also prospered in the town. North Dakota entered the Union in 1889 as a dry state. However, until the 18th Amendment, Minnesota was wet, and so enterprising Fargoans brought patrons over the river to saloons in jag wagons, before taking them back to the red light district in Fargo.

Three months after his solo trans-Atlantic flight, "Lucky Lindy," Charles Lindbergh, landed near Hector Field in Fargo. His visit in August 1927 was attended by thousands, as he drove in a motorcade to the El Zagal Bowl where he gave a speech that was broadcast by WDAY. The arrival of such a national hero in Fargo was a cause for city-wide rejoicing. (David Smith)

As in most towns, parades provided good, cheap entertainment and were well-attended. Note the wooden sidewalks and dirt streets in this late-nineteenth century photograph. (NDIRS, 51.40.15)

Work Horse Parade
Fargo N.Dak.

Fargoans paid tribute to the workhorse in this 1923 parade. Though they were doomed by automobiles, workhorses continued to draw most dairy wagons and some lumber and coal wagons into the 1930s. (NDIRS, 57.40.13)

Spring is always very welcome in Fargo after the long hard winter. In 1940, the city decided to celebrate its arrival by holding a Lilac Day. (SHSND, 0075-460)

At the other end of the summer, the NDAC Homecoming has always been a big event for Fargo. In the 1920s, the day started with a parade typified by inventiveness and fun in all participants, like these students dressed as chewing gum in 1929. The parade was followed by a bison barbecue at Dacotah Field, a football game, and then dancing at Festival Hall. (NDIRS, AHo 54)

Fargo schools took the lead in organized sports in the city. This hockey team from Fargo Central played teams from Moorhead, Valley City, and Detroit Lakes. (NDIRS, 2070.290.4)

NDAC also had organized sports, including boxing. This bout, staged in 1931, was held in the campus armory, better known as Festival Hall. Boxing was an intercollegiate sport in the 1920s and 1930s. (NDIRS, ABo)

NDAC did not have a theater until Professor of English and Oratory, Alfred G. Arvold, persuaded the administration to convert the unused chapel at the top of Old Main. A stage, proscenium arch, and 200 seats were installed. Thus was born the Little Country Theatre, dedicated in 1914. By the mid-1920s, theater operations had expanded to occupy much of the second and third floors of Old Main. (NDIRS, BLi 77-042.2)

In 1923, the Lincoln Log Cabin addition was made to the theater complex in Old Main. This was used for entertaining, banquets, and theatrical productions. Early in 1943, renowned opera singer Marian Anderson was the guest of honor at one such event. (NDIRS, BLi 77-L56.4)

In the early years of the city, good hunting in Fargo was a much-publicized recreation. In this 1876 photograph, a bird-hunting couple in matching attire poses beside a Northern Pacific observation car just west of town. (NDIRS, 2029.8.47)

The first 18-hole golf course in North Dakota opened at the Fargo Country Club in 1923, with the completion of nine holes along the Red River. The other nine holes had been constructed several years earlier on the southern edge of town. (NDIRS, 51.139.1)

Fargo lacked the topography to develop downhill skiing and thus take maximum advantage of its cold and snowy winters. To rectify this problem, the Dovre Ski Club arranged to build a ski jump west of the county poor farm, now Trollwood Park. Merchants contributed the materials and the Federal Emergency Relief Administration contrubuted the labor, and in 1935 the 140-foot-high, 300-foot-long jump opened. A good jump would take the skier 170 feet, to the banks of the Red River from where he or she could glide over into Minnesota. (NDIRS, 51.184.1)

Much easier than ski-jumping, skating has always been a popular winter pastime in Fargo. These skaters enjoy the fresh air at a temporary rink near Island Park, a gift to the city from the Northern Pacific Railroad in 1878. (NDIRS, 2029.8.42)

The ski jump was extremely popular with Fargo residents. Ruth Landfield remembers one of her father's best friends, Ole Olson, still skiing the jump at the age of 103. The jump was dismantled in the 1940s because it posed a hazard to air traffic. (SHSND, 0075-445a)

During the summer months, the Red River was the site of much recreation. The stretch of river through Fargo had several places to rent boats, and shooting the dam was a popular pastime, as seen here in 1920. (NDIRS, 2022.2.5)

Concrete banks and diving boards were installed to make a swimming area by Dommer's Boathouse on the Red River,. This proved very popular, especially with the boys of the town. (SHSND, 0075-564)

When good weather finally reaches Fargo, its citizens like to spend as much of the time as possible outdoors. The large number of parks in the city, like Oak Grove Park, pictured here, helps to make this possible. (David Smith)

From its inception as a land grant institution, the NDAC admitted women students as well as men. Here some young women enjoy a warm spring day on campus. In the background are Old Main and Ceres Hall. (NDIRS, ACa 54-I.22)

Paddling pools made Fargo parks attractive to young children and their mothers. (SHSND, A5962)

Automobile access to parks became increasingly vital as the city expanded its geographic limits, but pedestrian access was not sacrificed.(SHSND, A5948)

Barnett Field was home to the Fargo-Moorhead Twins, the town's first baseball team and a Fargo institution for over twenty years. The stadium stood on the site of North High School and was built with Works Progress Administration labor in 1936. It was demolished in the 1960s after the contraction of minor league baseball doomed the team. (SHSND, 0075-577)

KVOX broadcast Twins games by the "Voice of the Twins," Manny Margett, who openly supported the team. When he disagreed with a call, he would crawl from the press box on to the stadium roof to argue with the umpire, while simultaneously broadcasting the game. In 1953 the Twins fielded their most famous player, Roger Maras, who changed his name to Maris when he made it to the big leagues. Bob Feller also played for the team briefly in the late 1930s. (David Smith)

Fargo had its fair share of illegal entertainment, including prostitution. Early Fargoans did not try to abolish prostitution, but rather generated city income by fining brothels a pre-determined amount. This house at 201 Third Street North, was owned by Malvina Massey, an African-American madam. Black entertainers visiting Fargo, who were frequently barred from hotels and boarding houses, usually ended up staying with Massey. (NDIRS, FHc, 106-2)

Purchasing alcohol was also illegal in North Dakota from 1889 until the end of national prohibition in 1933. However, until 1919, drinking was still legal in Minnesota. Therefore, enterprising Fargoans transported patrons to and from Moorhead saloons in jag wagons. (NDIRS, 328.1.34)

For legal adult entertainment, Fargo offered the Winter Garden, later renamed the Crystal Ballroom. In 1928, R.E. (Doc) Chinn leased the city auditorium and opened it for dances. Many great names played there, including Duke Ellington and Louis Armstrong. One of the jobs of

Fargo policewoman Alice Duffy was to check the ages of the women dancing and make sure than no one danced too close. The ballroom closed in the late 1950s. (NDIRS, 51.131.2)

Fargoans staged their own dancing entertainment. These young novice tap dancers attended the Early School of Dance, owned by Jane Marie Early (in the center). (NDIRS, 51.112.22)

Some local performers made it big. Virginia Bruce was born in Minneapolis in 1910, but grew up in Fargo. Bruce made her movie debut in 1928 and went on to be a popular leading lady of the 1930s and 1940s. She starred opposite such actors as James Stewart, William Powell, and James Cagney. Bruce died in California in 1982. (NDIRS, 2043.2.1)

With the advent of movies, Fargo, like all other towns, built motion picture palaces. The leading one was the Fargo Theater, built in 1925. At the time it was a state-of-the-art silent movie house, with an elaborate Wurlitzer pipe organ and fully-operational stage for vaudeville shows. Redesigned in the 1930s in the popular art deco style, the theater is still alive and well today. (NDIRS, 51.171.1)

Another theater, the State on NP Avenue, was not so lucky, and did not survive past the heyday of moving pictures and the expansion of commerce away from the downtown area. (NDIRS, 51.26.14)

The Texas Ranger poses for an advertising shot for his performance on WDAY radio. The pile of letters on the table in the foreground is meant to indicate this rustic violinist's popularity. (David Smith)

In 1922, WDAY became the first licensed radio station in the northwest. Its new transmitter building on Main Avenue in West Fargo opened in 1932. WDAY, an early member of the National Broadcasting Company's network, has consistently brought news and entertainment to the Fargo area. (NDIRS, 2023.33.5)

Another musician poses for WDAY. The caption on the postcard reads, "For Health and Happiness, Go-Far Old Timer." WDAY combed the local area for home-grown talent. (David Smith)

The State Fair was held at the fairgrounds in Fargo every other year. An important component of the fair was the Women's and Art Building pictured here. Women's clubs, such as the Fargo Woman's Club founded in 1884, had been active in city life since the early days. The goals of these clubs usually involved cultural uplift and social improvement. (NDIRS, 51.48.19)

The state fair was a place for spectacle as well as culture. In 1908, this airship, the first in North Dakota, made several flights during the fair, attracting thousands of spectators. (NDIRS, 459.1.2)

Tired out by their day at the fair, this curiously somber mother and daughter pose for a souvenir photograph commemorating their visit to Fargo. (David Smith)

www.ingramcontent.com/pod-product-compliance
Lightning Source LLC
Chambersburg PA
CBHW080630110426
42813CB00006B/1644